Ramblin' Rudy
A Could-be-for-True Dog Story

Michael E. Owens
Illustrations by Leda Owens

Published by Scribblers Press
9741 SW 174th Place Road
Summerfield, Florida 34491

Printed by Trinity Press
3190 Reps Miller Road, Suite 360,
Norcross, Georgia 30071

Copyright © 2021 Michael E. Owens
All rights reserved.

Illustrated by Leda Owens
Layout by Bridgett Joyce
Edit by Casey Daniels
Text set in Times New Roman

Printed in U.S.A.

Library of Congress Control Number: 2020912609
Owens, Michael E., 5/28/2020
Ramblin' Rudy – A Could-be-for-True Dog Story / Michael E. Owens
Summary: Rudy was someone's dog in South Louisiana before he got lost and was picked up and became a rescue dog. This is his could-be-for-true dog story before the Owens's got him.

ISBN: 978-1-950308-26-2

Contact Information
www.BooksbyMEO.com and www.scribblersweb.com

Ordering Information
For ordering this book and other books by Michael E. Owens, check page 40.

Disclaimer
This is a work of fiction. Any resemblance to actual events or persons, living or dead, is entirely coincidental.

Readability Statistics

Words	5,489
Characters	24,674
Paragraphs	229

Sentences	381
Flesch Reading Ease	79
Flesch-Kincaid Grade Level	5

Dedication

To all the devoted and enthusiastic
individuals who care enough for out furry
friends to rescue them from certain demise.
I am grateful for those special individuals
in Baton Rouge, Louisiana and particularly
grateful for the APAWS organization
for saving Rudy for us.

Thank you,
Mr. and Mrs. Owens

Acknowledgements

Thanks to my wife Leda Owens for her artwork in this book and all the previous books in which she has meticulously provided such outstanding illustrations. She has worked diligently and passionately to excel at her craft.

Also, I am grateful for Casey Daniels who has expertly edited her fourth book for me. Her constant attention to detail has, again, made my book better than I could have on my own. Her encouraging spirit has been a blessing.

Of course, Bridgett Joyce continues to surprise me with her insight and expertise by preparing my books with such clarity and attractiveness - always going above and beyond my expectations. The final product is a tribute to her professionalism and Godly character.

Many thanks to Charles de Andrade and the Scribblers Christian Writers Group for their support and for giving me a means to promote my books and provide the resources to get them to my readers. His leadership has shown how the providence of God has led us in our endeavors to praise Him.

Also, we want to thank our next door neighbor, Ms. Julie, a true dog lover and our very own dog sitter. She has been faithfully watching our dogs since 2015 whenever we have had to travel to attend book fairs and festivals to market our books. Our dogs love her, especially Rudy, and she loves them back. Thank you Ms, Julie for always being there for us and our dogs.

Last but not least, we want to thank our grandkids for contributing their art to this book. Each were asked to draw a picture of Rudy for the Gallery. Thanks, kiddos for doing a great job. We love you.

M.E.O.

TABLE OF CONTENTS

Chapter   **Page**

Introduction 4
What's Your Story about Your Rescue Pet? 5
1 - At Home in the Morning 7
2 - Chasing Chickens Out in the Yard 9
3 - Fried Eggs 11
4 - Going to School – NOT! 12
5 - Newspaper Delivery 15
6 - The Meat Market 17
7 - The Cute Dachshund 19
8 – The Cajun Fisherman 21
9 – School's Out 23
10 – What Happened at Home? 25
11 - Alone 27
12 – The Pound 29
13 – The Rescue 31
14 – A New People Family 33
Gallery of Rudy's Photos 35
Other Titles Available from Michael E. Owens 37
How to Order Books by Michael E. Owens 38
Michael E. Owens – the Author 39
Want a visit from a Published Author? 40
Up Coming Books by Michael E. Owens .... Back cover

Ramblin' Rudy
A Could-be-for-True Dog Story

Introduction - A Rescue Dog

Rudy is a real dog. He was found roaming the streets of a small town in southern Louisiana. A dog catcher picked him up and took him to a pound. His owner was never located. This pound was very overcrowded with many dogs and cats. They could not take care of them all. So, a group of people who really love dogs and want to find new owners for them, took Rudy to Baton Rouge, Louisiana. Rudy was now what is called a "rescue dog." The people who rescued Rudy put his picture on a website for people to find rescued dogs. A lady named Mrs. Owens saw him and fell in love with him. Before you knew it, Rudy was adopted by Mr. and Mrs. Owens. That is where our true story begins.

Before the Owens' adopted Rudy, they could only imagine what his life was like. Who was his owner? Where did he live? Did the owners take good care of him? Were they sad that he was gone?

Now, Rudy is a very happy dog who really loves people. Mr. Owens, who had already written several children's books, decided he would write a book about Rudy. It would be a story – a could-be-for-true story - about Rudy's life before the Owens's got him.

What's Your Story about Your Rescue Pet?

Do you have a rescued pet you could tell a story about – a could-be-for-true story? Try writing your rescued pet's story like Mr. Owens did with Rudy. Use your imagination. What great exciting exploits did your pet have? Maybe your rescued pet had traveled around the world, or maybe your pet was a crime fighter, or saved a kitten from a burning building or maybe he or she had unknown super-powers. It's your pet and your story. Tell your "could-be-for-true story" however you like. Mr. Owens did, and this is his rescued pet's story.

Chapter 1

At Home in the Morning

Mr. Taylor loved Rudy. He had Rudy ever since he was a puppy; ever since Mrs. Taylor had gotten him from some neighbors several years earlier. Rudy became very protective of Mrs. Taylor. If Mr. Taylor got too close to his wife, Rudy would bark and growl. Mr. Taylor thought it was cute, but he respected Mrs. Taylor's space – and Rudy's.

Rudy was still a pup when Mrs. Taylor passed away. Without his wife at home, Mr. Taylor became lonely. He could tell that Rudy missed her too. Slowly they became closer, and Rudy didn't bark nor growl at Mr. Taylor anymore.

Before he would let Rudy out in the morning, Mr. Taylor put out a bowl of dog food and a fresh bowl of water. He knew Rudy would ignore it. All Rudy wanted to do was to get out of the house, take care of his "business" and head out for his everyday routine. Yes, Rudy had established a daily routine for visiting his neighborhood. Mr. Taylor had a fence – a good one – but Rudy was a master of escape. He could always find the smallest opening and off he would go. Since Rudy managed to come back every afternoon, Mr. Taylor didn't worry too much about him.

Mr. Taylor was getting very old, and he could barely keep up with a frisky dog like Rudy.

Chapter 2
Chasing Chickens Out in the Yard

Mr. Taylor only had a few animals on his property now. Many years ago, he had a big farm, with cows, horses, goats, and pigs, but now that he was older, he only kept his chickens and a rabbit in a large cage. The chicken were easy to feed, as was the rabbit. He would get eggs from the chickens. The rabbit? Well, he just liked rabbits.

The first order of business Rudy took care of every morning was to aggravate the chickens. Mr. Taylor had raised chickens all his life and he tried to stop Rudy from riling up his chickens every morning, but it was no use. Rudy was determined to have some fun before he got on his way. He would make a beeline straight toward them as they pecked at the ground around their coop. It was a sight to see him chase those chickens as they squawked and screeched, flitting around the yard, sending feathers scattering across their pen. Rudy never ever caught one, and he probably wouldn't know what to do with it if he did. After a good chase of the chickens, Rudy would bark at the rabbit, just to get him stirred up. Rudy could not get to him, since he was already caged, but the rabbit was not smart enough to figure that out and would run circles around the inside of his cage when Rudy would appear. One thing Rudy had learned he would not do (ever) was to chase the duck nor the cats. Previous encounters proved they were not animals to be messed with. He could still remember the cat's swat across his nose and the ducks biting at his tail.

Once all was in order at home, a squeeze through the gate and Rudy was off for his daily adventures.

Chapter 3
Fried Eggs

Ms. Alice lived next door. Most people would say that Ms. Alice was a frail woman. She was older, thin, and looked fragile. But then, she would be seen with her dogs and she had no problem taking care of even the biggest of them. Ms. Alice did not walk her dogs anymore, but Rudy had heard that she used to take six or more out a couple times a day. Once Rudy remembered her taking him and two other dogs out for a walk. It was just three of them but what a mess! She spent an hour untangling their leashes.

Rudy liked her and this was always his first stop. Ever since he was a pup, when Mr. and Mrs. Taylor would need to travel, even for a few hours, Ms. Alice would take Rudy in and watch him while they were gone. Ms. Alice did this for lots of folks and their dogs (but no cats of course!). Somehow, Rudy became her favorite. No one is quite sure how this happened. To prove it, every morning Ms. Alice would fry an egg just for Rudy. She claimed he loved it – and he did. Everyone who had ever heard of this had questions for Ms. Alice and Rudy.

"Ms. Alice, how did you find out Rudy likes fried eggs so much in the first place?"

"Rudy, how did you let Ms. Alice know you like fried eggs in the first place?"

Both would just smile and go on. (If truth be told, Ms. Alice had accidentally splatted a fried egg on the floor, and before she could clean it up, Rudy had eaten it and licked the spot clean!)

Of course, getting a fried egg every morning at Ms. Alice's house did not come without some responsibility. You see, not only did Ms. Alice watch other people's dogs, but she also had some of her own. Her house was always full of dogs of all breeds, colors, and sizes. It was her own dogs that caused the most problems though. They were three schipperkes named Lester, North, and Lewis, and were they loud! They loved to get out in the yard first thing in the morning and head straight for the garden to dig and dig and dig in the soft dirt.

Watching Ms. Alice chase them out every day gave Rudy an idea to help. He would chase them out too, and he got pretty good at it. Soon, that fried egg would become his reward for a job well done.

"You are a very smart dog!" Ms. Alice would say.

Once he felt he had controlled the garden situation at Ms. Alice's house (and finished eating his fried egg, of course), Rudy moved onto more serious endeavors.

Chapter 4
Going to School - NOT!

Rudy could not tell time, but something told him every day when it was time for school. Now, Rudy didn't actually go to school. He did try a few times to prance into the building but got chased away by a secretary.

The children were gathering at the corner, waiting for Ms. Anderson, the crossing guard, to let them cross the street. Rudy had learned a very good lesson a long time ago – DO NOT CROSS THE STREET BY YOURSELF! Plus, with all the kids at the crosswalk, he got a lot of attention with pats, strokes, hugs, and an occasional kiss. He liked all that. After Ms. Anderson blew her whistle, all the kids started walking and Rudy joined in.

Ms. Anderson looked at Rudy and said, "You are a very smart dog!"

He followed them to the front of the school and stopped. There, he got more pats, strokes, hugs, and an occasional kiss from the kids getting off the buses. He knew not to get too close to the front of the school. School secretaries are not very nice. Soon, only a few kids were left heading into the school. Occasionally one or two would pass by and give him a quick pat. He always enjoyed attention.

Chapter 5
Newspaper Delivery

After making sure all the kids got to school safely, Rudy could start his rounds for the day. It started with a visit to Mr. Robertson's house. He was a tall, lanky man; always clean-shaven and neat. About the time Mr. Robertson would be walking out his front door to get his morning paper, Rudy would be walking by his house. For a long time, Mr. Robertson would see Rudy and greet him with a wave which, in a few months, turned into a wave with a head scratch which, a few months later still, turned into a wave with a head scratch and a treat, which sometimes included a brief conversation. Rudy had no idea what Mr. Robertson was talking about, but he really enjoyed the treats anyway. In a moment, Mr. Robertson would pick up his paper and go back into the house, waving bye to Rudy.

One day Rudy passed Mr. Robertson's house, but there was no Mr. Robertson. There was a paper, but no Mr. Robertson. Rudy looked at the front door, then looked at the paper, then back at the front door, then at the paper. And then, all of a sudden the front door opened, but something was different. Mr. Robertson was not standing up—he was sitting in a chair with large wheels on the side, too big to fit through the front door. Mr. Robertson spoke, "Rudy, can you bring me my paper?"

Rudy saw him reach out the door, but he couldn't pick up the paper. Immediately, Rudy realized what Mr. Robertson wanted. Rudy grabbed the paper between his teeth and bought it to Mr. Robertson.

"Thank you, Rudy!" Mr. Robertson said. "You are a very smart dog."

From that day on, Rudy would bring the paper to Mr. Robertson's front door and wait patiently for his wave, pat on the head, and a treat, and maybe a little conversation. Rudy then moved on to the big treat of the day.

Chapter 6
The Meat Market

When Rudy followed the streets past all of the houses, there were a lot of businesses. There was only one stop for Rudy at these places. It was Tony's Meat Market. Rudy has been coming here since he was a tiny pup. Back when Mr. Taylor could walk better, he would put a leash on Rudy, and they would walk there together to get meat. And each time without fail, Mr. Tony would give Rudy a small bone to chew. Later, when Mr. Taylor could not walk so easily, Mr. Tony would have someone deliver the meat. When after a while Mr. Taylor stopped ordering meat, Rudy missed the small chew bone. No matter how much time had passed, Rudy never forgot the way to Mr. Tony's.

"You are a very smart dog," Mr. Tony would say. Mr. Tony was a large, round man with a black beard and a very bushy mustache. He always had a big smile and he seemed to laugh a lot. Rudy liked him from the very first time; not just for the treat, of course.

Still to this day, he always had a bone for Rudy. Sometimes it was a big bone –more than enough for one dog or even two. With that big bone in his mouth, Rudy found another stop on his morning jaunt.

Chapter 7
The Cute Dachshund

One day, soon after Rudy found his way to Mr. Tony's by himself, he got his treat and headed home. On his way home he would pass Ms. Schultz' house. She was a tall, rather large woman who must have kept the cleanest house ever. She was always sweeping and mopping. She seemed to really enjoy seeing Rudy pass by. She would have a big smile and would talk in a loud, deep voice. She would always say, *"Sie sind ein kluger Hund!"* Rudy had no idea she was telling him in German, "You are a smart dog."

She never had a dog before until that day, Rudy noticed she brought home a Dachshund. She was a little girl with a shiny brown coat and big brown eyes. Rudy thought she was beautiful. He learned her name was Fraun. He could tell she needed a friend. Ever since that first day they met, Rudy would share his bone with her.

Almost three months later, she had five little pups following behind her. They were small at first and didn't care for the bone, but as they got bigger, the bone was a tasty treat they could all enjoy. Ms. Shultz seemed to love her new dog family.

Ms. Schultz thought Rudy was so sweet to the pups and so clever. *"Sie sind ein kluger Hund!"* she would always say.

Chapter 8
The Cajun Fisherman

Rudy would always leave his bone with Fraun and her family. He had another stop, and he didn't need to bring a bone for this one.

This was Mr. Richard (reè-shard). At first Rudy did not like Mr. Richard. He was a crusty old man. He had a big boat in his back yard. It was old, had peeling paint and a big hole in the bottom. Mr. Richard had a black patch over one eye and a wooden stick for part of one leg and a white boot over the other. He had lots of graying whiskers; and he always seemed to wear dirty clothes that smelled just like rotten fish.

He was not someone Rudy thought he could ever enjoy visiting. Rudy would make a wide walk around Mr. Richard's place whenever he was sitting in his backyard cleaning lots of fish. Mr. Richard would try to talk to Rudy, but his voice was strange.

"Hey dawg," Mr. Richard would say, "wat ju name, lil' puppy?" Mr. Richard always called him 'lil' puppy.' "Come he'a. I gots sum tasty fish for youse. Oo wee, 'lil' puppy; is good, cher!"

Rudy never ate fish before, and it did not seem so tempting at first.

It was probably a month of walking by Mr. Richard's before Rudy even slowed down to inspect Mr. Richard's backyard. Then it was another month before Rudy would stop and sniff. But before long, Rudy would start to get a little closer and closer to Mr. Richard – until he was close enough for a head pat. Occasionally Mr. Richard would have a shark to clean. No one else would eat it but Mr. Richard, and he would share some with Rudy. It didn't take long before Rudy developed a taste for shark meat. Mr. Richard liked sharing with Rudy. "Youse a very smart lil puppy, ma cher," Mr. Richard would say.

Chapter 9
School's Out

From Mr. Richard's house Rudy was close enough to hear the school bell in the afternoon. He knew it was time to head for home and help the students cross the street. Of course, it also meant a time for more pats, strokes, hugs, and occasional kisses. Rudy thought if he could go to school, he would get pats, strokes, hugs, and occasional kisses all day long. Ms. Anderson never gave Rudy a pat, or stroke, or hug, or an occasional kiss. She was busy holding the stop sign with one hand and getting the kids across the street with the other.

But this day, something different happened. Ms. Anderson heard a loud siren and stopped the children from crossing. She even made them stand back, away from the street. It was an ambulance with a loud blaring siren, speeding down the street. Just as it was about to reach the corner, one of the little girls continued to walk into the street. Immediately Rudy barked loudly and, grabbing the hem of her coat, pulled her back. Once it passed, Ms. Anderson stopped the traffic and let everyone cross, including Rudy. As he passed Ms. Anderson, she looked down at Rudy and, with a pat on the head, said, "You are a very smart dog, Rudy."

Chapter 10

What Happened at Home?

Just like every other day, it was afternoon when Rudy was heading home to see Mr. Taylor. Every day when Rudy got there, Mr. Taylor was always sitting on the front porch in the swing waiting for him. Mr. Taylor would move it slowly back and forth; just slow enough for Rudy to jump on it and climb onto Mr. Taylor's lap. Rudy had had a great day. He had seen all his friends, got some nice treats (Rudy really loved getting treats!), and a whole lot of pats, strokes, hugs, and occasional kisses. Now he was ready for a nice afternoon nap, all snuggled in Mr. Taylor's lap.

As Rudy approached his house, he noticed the ambulance had stopped on his street. As Rudy got closer, he realized it had stopped in front of his house! Rudy froze when suddenly two men came out of his house carrying Mr. Taylor on a bed. Rudy felt very confused when they put the bed in the back of the ambulance and then drove off.

They can't take Mr. Taylor! thought Rudy. He began to chase after the ambulance, as fast as he could run. He kept running for as long as he could; down many streets and through many turns. The ambulance kept getting farther and farther away. He ran and ran until he couldn't see the ambulance anymore. He did not know where they took Mr. Taylor. On top of that, Rudy had no idea where he was or how to get back home. Slowly, with his head down, Rudy just kept walking and walking. He did not know where to go. He passed many homes, then many businesses and other places until there were nothing left except trees and a lonely road. There was no one there that knew him. No one there to say, "You are a very smart dog, Rudy."

Chapter 11
Alone

Rudy could not remember how long he was on the road. It could have been hours. It could have been days. Suddenly, a van pulled up in front of him and stopped. A friendly-faced man stepped out. Rudy liked friendly faces and ran to him immediately. He picked up Rudy, which seemed to be a good thing, but then he tossed him in a crate in the back of the van. He was not alone. There were other dogs as well. None of them seemed to be happy they were in the van. There was so much barking and whining and whimpering. Little did they know that the place they were going was worse than the van.

Chapter 12
The Pound

When the van stopped, the dogs, including Rudy, were placed in cages in an animal shelter. There were many dogs and cats there. It was loud and it smelled strange. Suddenly Rudy realized he was hungry. He wasn't sure how long it had been since he last ate. Soon, a bowl of food was shoved into his crate. It was not the treats he had been used to eating, but it was food and he gobbled it down.

Rudy had never been locked up before. He wanted to visit with his friends and be with Mr. Taylor. No chickens to chase in here. No fried egg to eat. He wanted to see the children who crossed the street every day for school. He was missing their pats, strokes, hugs, and occasional kisses. Who is going to bring Mr. Robertson his paper? My bones! Fraun! Mr. Richard! Rudy was overcome with what he should be doing – not locked up in a cage! He began to whimper.

Chapter 13
The Rescue

After the next few days, he saw some ladies walking up and down the aisle, looking at all the dogs. Somehow Rudy sensed this was a good thing. Maybe it would be his way out. The thought perked up Rudy a bit. As they approached his crate, he decided to put on his best "take-me-I'm cute-I'm the one for you" act, by wagging his tail, cocking his head, and running around in little circles. He did it, and it worked. To make a long story short, Rudy had found a foster parent who took him so he could be adopted. Little did Rudy know at the time, but those people saved Rudy's life.

The first thing the foster parents did was take Rudy to the veterinarian for a thorough checkup. Then they took his picture, making sure he looked as cute as could be for the new, soon-to-be parents. They put that picture on the internet website. It didn't take long before Rudy caught the eye of Mrs. Owens. She said to herself, "Rudy looks like a very smart dog."

Chapter 14

A New People Family

Well, that's the end of Rudy's "could-be-for-true dog story." From this point on, it's Rudy's "true dog story." Rudy was picked up by Mrs. Owens from the foster family and he soon became a wonderful member of the Owens family. Soon after, the family moved to Georgia and by that time, Rudy had two more little "brothers," Hershey and Walie, and one very large, Great Dane "sister," named Ella.

Here is a picture of Rudy. He is a poodle mix, with a light brown coat and weighs about 20 pounds. He still loves to be a lap dog. Now he has Mr. Owens' lap to use. Rudy still loves to eat his treats and Mrs. Owens makes sure he has lots of varieties and never runs out. And, of course, he still gets lots of pats, strokes, hugs, and occasional kisses.

This is a picture of him in his new yard. It is very spacious, and he loves roaming around the many trees, bushes, and flowers throughout the yard. The yard also has many trails which the whole dog family enjoys.

Rudy is still making friends. Ginger, a miniature pinscher, and occasionally, her two visiting dachshund cousins, Rupert, and Quagmire, live in the house on the left with Ms. Kay. His friends to the right are Brody, an Australian shepherd, George, a black lab, and Squirt, a Heinz 57, all who live with Ms. Julie and Mr. Chuck. Across the street from Ms. Julie and Mr. Chuck lives Mr. Aaron and Ms. Mandy who are owned by Elliot, a rescued pit bull-Dachshund mix. Moose, the other dog, was found in the deep, deep woods by Mr. Aaron while he was hunting for wild boar. He appears to be a beagle-corgi mix. Moose hasn't really said, but he is happy with Ms. Mandy and Mr. Aaron. On the corner is a yard full of schipperkes who own Mr. and Mrs. Smith. Rudy loves being around other dog lovers as well.

So that's the story for a very special rescued dog named Rudy – the "could-be-for-true dog story" and the "true dog story"!

When people meet him they still say, "You are a very smart dog, Rudy."

Gallery of Rudy Photos

Austin age 14

Gage age 6

Gale age 7

Gem age 12

Gear age 3

Remy age 3

Rain age 9

Aurora age 13

Ever age 7

True age 11

Logan age 7

Other Titles Available from Michael E. Owens Available from Scribblersweb.com and Amazon

The I Hate Vegetables Book of Poetry for Kids

The "I Hate Vegetables Book of Poetry for Kids" is a fun, whimsical and irreverent look at the veggies kids hate to eat the most. It's a book to be enjoyed by those who hate vegetables as well as those who love them! Please – read and be entertained! (and eat your veggies!)

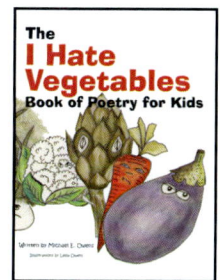

Does the River Ever End?

It's the 1840s along the Mississippi River and Mike Fink must live in the shadow of his infamous father, with no one giving him a fair shake. Mike and a slave, Cletus, believing they will be charged for two murders on the riverboat, escape capture through the backwoods of Illinois, heading as far away as they can. Being chased by the law and outlaws too, will they finally make it to freedom?

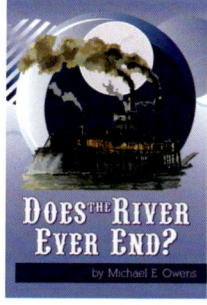

Summer of Heroes

In the 1870's, Billy looks forward to a lazy summer in West Texas, waiting for his dad to return to take their cattle to market. When he doesn't return, the task of trail boss lands in his lap. On his travels with the herd, he gains an unexpected trail hand runs into a band of rustlers, Mr. Chisholm, Bass Reeves, and a famous Indian chief in Oklahoma. On his return home, he goes after his dream – a wild stallion in the hills. Billy never considered himself a hero, but others had a different idea.

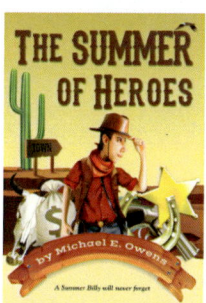

Ordinary People - Extraordinary God
Vol 1 and Vol 2

The first two books in this series of drama presentations include nine skits each involving unnamed characters in the Bible who were instrumental in spreading the Gospel of Jesus Christ.

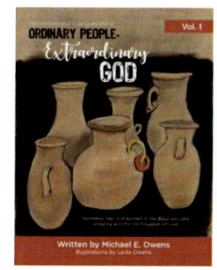 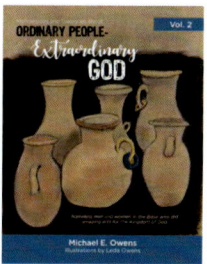

Coming Soon!

The Happy Life of a Possum Named Owen

Owen and his numerous brothers and sisters learn many lessons from Mama possum. Although Owen thinks he is the bravest, he is the last to leave home with more lessons to learn on his own.

Eggs! Eggs! Eggs!

The forest animals, who paint the Easter eggs, became overwhelmed. Their new invention seems to be the answer until it is stolen! A wonderful musical for younger grades and special needs.

Ms. Mouse Wants a New House

Where is the best place for a mouse to live? In a busy city? In an office tower? In the suburbs?

How to order books written by Michael E. Owens

Mr. Owens has books for Children, Tweens, Young Adults and for Adults. If interested in purchasing any of his books, you may order them on-line either from Scribblers Press or from Amazon (Check availability of books on Amazon. Some may also be available as E-books.)

SCRIBBLERS
Go to **www.scribblersweb.com**
Click on the Menu Bar in upper left corner.
Click on Authors.
Click on the author, Michael E. Owens.
Find the book(s) and add to your cart.
Follow the on-screen instructions for purchasing and shipping.
While on Scribblers, check out Mr. Owens' podcasts and videos.

AMAZON
Books can be ordered from Amazon by going on-line to **www.amazon.com**
Open www.amazon.com
Type name of book in "Search"
Find the book(s) and add to your cart.
Follow the on-screen instructions for purchasing and shipping.
While on Internet, check out Mr. Owens' podcasts and You Tube videos.

> **Children, please consult your parents before ordering any books on-line.**

Readability Statistics for "Ramblin' Rudy: A Could-be for True Dog Story"

Words	5,489	Sentences	381
Characters	24,674	Flesch Reading Ease	79
Paragraphs	229	Flesch-Kincaid Grade Level	5

Michael E. Owens, the Author

Michael E. Owens has enjoyed writing most of his life, beginning with his junior high school days living in New Orleans. While in high school, he won the Journalism Gold Medal Award for writing. In college, he was given recognition for his writing on historical topics and was voted "Best Actor" his senior year.

Mike is married to the lovely Leda Still. In 2018 they published their third book together entitled, "The I Hate Vegetables Book of Poetry for Kids". They have also released Volume 1 and 2 of an adult drama book series entitled, "Ordinary People – Extraordinary God". Volumes 3 and 4 will be coming out in 2021. "The Bird Nest Real Estate Agency" is their sixth book. Coming soon, "The Happy Life of a Possum Named Owen," "Ms. Mouse Wants a New House," "Eggs! Eggs! Eggs!," and "Ramblin' Rudy" are four additional children's books to be ready for early 2021.

Before the Covid-19 pandemic of '20-'21, Mike and Leda had volunteered at the Southeastern Railway Museum for several years, with Leda in the gift shop, and Mike working with the Second Thursday Preschool Program. During the Christmas holidays they were Santa and Mrs. Claus for the "Breakfast and Lunch with Santa" programs at the Museum and worked at the Plaza las Americas mall. In addition, they served at the Scottish Rite Children's Hospital on Christmas Day handing out presents to the young patients, as well as many other events during the season. Also, they recently directed all-senior cast plays at the Bethesda Senior Center, in Lawrenceville, Georgia and at the Adult Recreation Center in Roswell, Georgia. In their spare time, Mike and Leda enjoyed square dancing several times a month as well as spending time with their four pooches and their 15 grandchildren.

Want a visit from a published children's author?

Mr. Owens is a retired teacher who had taught special education for most of his adult teaching career. He has a background in teaching, speech, acting, directing and sign language. As a published writer of children's books, and skilled as a carnival clown for many years, Mr. Owens has a unique perspective on education with experience as a supervisor, teacher, actor, director, playwright and writer.

Mr. Owens has visited numerous schools to share his storytelling skills, his humor, and his expertise to encourage students to become writers. He has an uncanny and refreshing ability to communicate, connect and motivate children of all ages.

He is available, free of charge, to visit classrooms, school libraries and other academic and community assemblies in face-to-face or virtual settings to share first-hand knowledge and experience of being an author and of the writing process.

To reserve Mr. Owens for your next event, you may contact him through his email at **MichaelEOwens47@gmail.com**.

He is looking forward to visiting your school, library, or other facility soon.

"An entertaining and highly charged presentation; if I have to say so myself."

M.E.O.